WOODLANDS

Michael Chinery

KINGFISHER BOOKS

A Woodland Walk

The well-worn woodland path emerges into a large clearing where fallow deer graze peacefully. Their eyes and ears are always alert for danger and the animals bolt for the safety of the trees as you approach. A jay and a chaffinch fly off noisily too, but the coal tit calmly goes on picking insects from the oak leaves. The large oaks at the edge of the clearing show signs of age: branches are dying and many have already fallen. Large bracket fungi, such as the dryad's saddle, grow on the trunks and weaken them still further. Many smaller bracket fungi grow on the dead stumps.

The woodland margin supports a fantastic variety of wildlife. The extra light at the edge of the wood encourages the growth of many more small plants than you will see in the shadowy centre. Flowers bloom throughout the spring and summer. Tree seedlings also sprout in the clearings but the deer give them little chance to grow. Deer don't like bracken, however, so this tall fern may spread rapidly. Hordes of insects enjoy the rich plant life. Butterflies sun themselves on the leaves and feed at the flowers. Hornets make their homes in hollow trees, while stag beetles and many others breed in the decaying stumps.

As you walk on down the path into the trees the ground gets damper. Clumps of male fern, looking like huge green shuttlecocks, replace the bracken and there are fewer flowers on the ground. A small stream trickles out of sight through the wood at the bottom of the slope. Many woodland animals come here to drink, leaving footprints for you to identify.

Beyond the stream the path rises up and skirts a pine plantation. The original oak woodland has been cut down to make way for the quick-growing conifers which provide much of our timber today. Sections of the plantation have recently been cleared and replanted with young trees. For a few years

The Country Code

1. Leave no litter.
2. Fasten all gates.
3. Avoid damaging fences, hedges and walls.
4. Guard against all fire risk.
5. Keep dogs under control.
6. Keep to paths across farmland.
7. Safeguard all water supplies.
8. Protect all forms of wildlife.
9. Go carefully on country roads.
10. Respect the life of the countryside.

A Woodland Walk

the young plantations are like woodland clearings with large numbers of flowers, insects and birds. Voles are also very common and often damage many of the young trees. The kestrel enjoys hunting here and is a good friend of the forester. The conifers are planted close together and as they grow they gradually cut out the light from the ground. Few plants can grow then and the animals are driven out. As you walk by the plantation you can see how dark it is. Even the lower branches are dead because there is no light.

The different types of woodland each have their own plants and animals for you to explore. Look carefully around you, and take a notebook in which to record your observations. A hand lens (x 10 is a good size) will also be useful for detailed examinations and a pair of binoculars (see page 24) for watching birds and mammals from a distance.

Woodland Types

The woodlands of Europe are of two main kinds – deciduous and evergreen. The deciduous trees drop their leaves in the autumn, but evergreens remain green throughout the year. Evergreen woods consist mainly of cone-bearing trees and most are found in colder regions – in the north and on the mountains. Deciduous forests contain different kinds of trees, but one kind is generally dominant. Look at your local woods and find out the kind of tree that occurs most. The kinds of trees growing in a wood depend largely on the type of soil.

Right: Beech trees cast deep shade and few plants can grow below them. Here a beech seedling is shooting up where a shaft of sunlight reaches the forest floor. One day it may grow large enough to replace one of the old trees of the forest. But very few seedlings ever get to this stage.

Above: Oak trees let plenty of light through to the woodland floor, even in summer, allowing bracken and many other plants to flourish.

An Oakwood

Most people can recognize oak trees by their leaves and their acorns, but did you know that we have two common species of oak? The pedunculate oak has stalked acorn cups and almost stalkless leaves, while the sessile oak has stalkless acorn cups and long stalks on its leaves. If you have oakwoods near your home, work out which kind of oak forms it. If you live in an upland area with relatively shallow soil you will probably find that the sessile oak is dominant. The pedunculate oak prefers to grow in the deeper soils of the valleys and the lowlands and is especially common on heavy clay. You can find both oaks together in many woods.

Oak trees come into leaf quite late in the spring, and even when in full leaf they do not cast a very deep shade. Lots of small plants can grow beneath them, especially on the deep rich soils of the pedunculate oakwoods. Some of the familiar flowers are shown on pages 18 and 19. Hazel grows everywhere in many oakwoods. It used to be cut to the ground every few years to provide slender poles for beansticks and hurdle-making. This system, known as coppicing, is still used in some woods, especially in nature reserves. It encourages flowering plants to spread over the ground, and the young stems sprouting from the cut stumps of the trees and shrubs provide plenty of cover for birds.

Ash trees are common in many oakwoods. They used to be coppiced like the hazel, and still are in some places. Their young trunks make excellent tool handles. Look for ash trees with several trunks rising up from a single base. These are trees which have been coppiced in the past and then allowed to grow up from the stumps. Pure ashwoods grow in some limestone districts.

A Beechwood

Beech trees, recognized by their very smooth bark and pointed buds (see page 6), like well-drained soils. The largest beechwoods in Britain are on the chalky and sandy soils of the south and east. Beech trees cast a very deep shade and few plants can survive underneath them. There might be drifts of bluebells in the spring, flowering and making their food before the beech leaves are fully open, but in the summer there is little but a thick layer of dead beech leaves. It is very much easier to walk through a beechwood than an oakwood.

Above: A natural pine forest in Scotland. Notice the well spaced trees. Plenty of light reaches through and allows heather to grow thickly below.

A Pinewood

You will have to go to northern regions or to the mountains to see natural pinewoods. The Scots pine is the commonest species. Look for the brick-red bark on its upper parts. It forms huge forests in parts of Scandinavia. Natural

Examining Owl Pellets

Owls swallow their prey whole, but they can't digest the fur and bones. When the flesh has been digested, the fur and bones are formed into a sausage-shaped pellet which is coughed up and spat out. Owls may produce two or three pellets in a day. Look for them under trees. Large numbers of pellets pile up under regular roosting places. The pellets are not smelly and if you pull them to pieces you can see what the owl has been eating. Stick the bones on a card and try to work out what parts of the body they came from. The triangular shoulder blades are easily identified. The prey animals are best identified by their skulls and jaws. Shrew teeth are sharply pointed and often tipped with red. Voles have long, chisel-like front teeth and a flat-topped wall of grinding teeth further back. Mouse skulls are similar, but the grinding teeth have more rounded surfaces. You can clean up the bones with the aid of tweezers and then bleach them by leaving them in hydrogen peroxide.

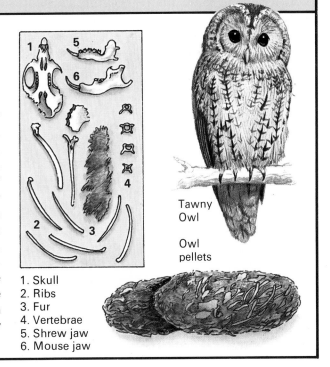

1. Skull
2. Ribs
3. Fur
4. Vertebrae
5. Shrew jaw
6. Mouse jaw

Tawny Owl

Owl pellets

5

Identifying Trees

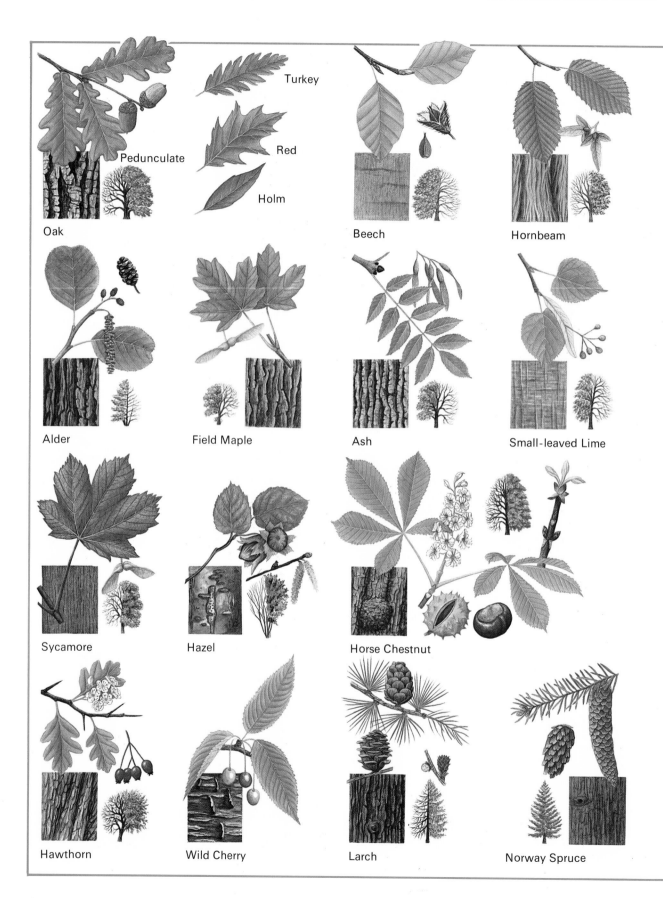

Oak

Turkey

Red

Holm

Pedunculate

Beech

Hornbeam

Alder

Field Maple

Ash

Small-leaved Lime

Sycamore

Hazel

Horse Chestnut

Hawthorn

Wild Cherry

Larch

Norway Spruce

Wych Elm

Silver Birch

Sweet Chestnut

False Acacia

Holly

Scots Pine

Yew

pinewoods are often quite open, with carpets of heather and bilberry bushes beneath the trees and birch trees mixed with them. The ground is covered with fungi in the autumn.

Other common cone-bearing trees include the spruces, with their long, sausage-shaped cones, and the larches. The latter are unusual conifers in that they drop their leaves in the autumn.

Identify the Trees

Some of the commoner woodland trees are illustrated here. Learning their leaf shapes is one of the best ways to identify them in the woods. The flowers and fruits are also very helpful, although they are not always present. Bark patterns will help you to recognize some species. The wild cherry, for example, is easily identified by its horizontal stripes and by the way in which the young bark flakes off in horizontal bands. The sweet chestnut has a spiral pattern on the lower part of the trunk. Look out, too, for the silvery bark and black triangles of the silver birch.

Examine the winter buds of deciduous trees. Their shapes and colours will help with

Grow a Horse Chestnut Bud

The winter buds of deciduous trees contain the next year's leaves, well wrapped up against the cold winds. The leaves start to expand and the buds burst open when the sap rises in the spring. Put a few twigs in water in early spring and watch the leaves unfold. It is best to use a large-leaved species like the horse chestnut seen here.

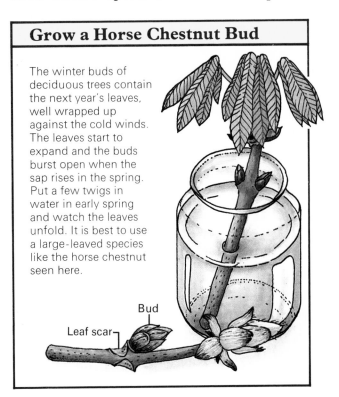

Bud

Leaf scar

Tree Projects

Finding the Height of a Tree

Two simple methods of estimating the height of a tree (or a building) are shown below.

Method 1: For this method you will need the help of a friend. Hold a ruler or a straight stick vertically in front of you and walk backwards or forwards until the stick appears to be exactly the same size as the tree: the bottom of the stick should coincide with the base of the tree and the top should appear level with the top of the tree. Keep your arm in the same position and swivel the stick until it is horizontal. Keep one end lined up with the base of the tree and ask your friend to walk along until he or she appears to be at the other end of the stick. Shout 'stop!' The distance from your friend to the base of the tree should equal the height of the tree.

Method 2: You can carry out this method by yourself. All you need is a straight stick *the same length* as the distance from your eye to your outstretched hand. Hold the stick upright at arm's length and move backwards or forwards until the stick coincides with the tree as in the first method. The distance from you to the base of the tree is then the same as the height of the tree. Pace out the distance or measure it with a long measuring tape.

You can test the accuracy of your measurements by testing these methods on a church tower or similar building of known height. Make a note of the tallest tree you can find. What kind is it? Did you know that some redwood trees in California are over 100 metres high?

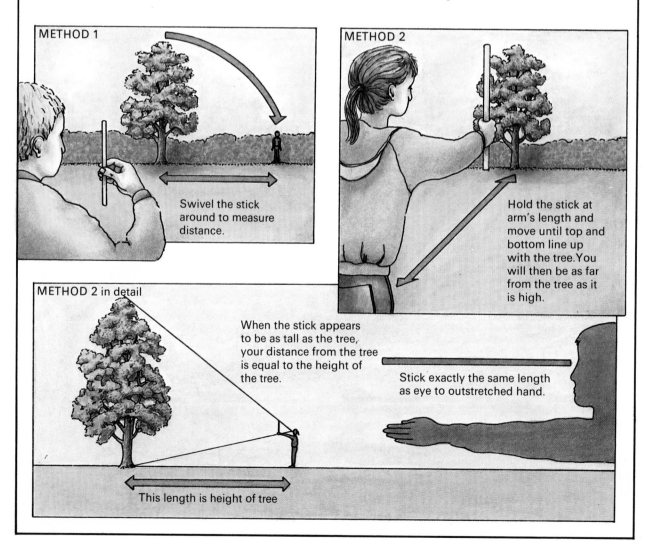

METHOD 1

Swivel the stick around to measure distance.

METHOD 2

Hold the stick at arm's length and move until top and bottom line up with the tree. You will then be as far from the tree as it is high.

METHOD 2 in detail

When the stick appears to be as tall as the tree, your distance from the tree is equal to the height of the tree.

Stick exactly the same length as eye to outstretched hand.

This length is height of tree

Tree Projects

Trees from Twigs

Small pieces of twig, known as cuttings, often grow roots if stuck in the soil, or even in a jar of water. Take cuttings from various trees and see which root most easily. Poplars and willows are very quick. Hawthorn is also a good tree to try. It is often better to pull off a shoot with a 'heel' than to cut it off.

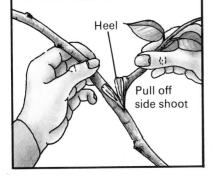

Heel

Pull off side shoot

Making Bark Rubbings

Look at the trunks of different kinds of trees and see how the bark patterns vary. Make a collection of the patterns by taking bark rubbings. You need some large sheets of fairly tough paper and a thick wax crayon. Some string may be useful for holding the paper on the tree, but a friend is better! Make sure that the paper can't move and then rub the crayon firmly over it. Watch how the bark pattern appears on the paper. Label the pattern with the name of the tree and keep it in your natural history collection. Fix one of the tree's leaves to the paper as well if you like.

The Age of a Tree

Find a tree that has recently been cut down and look at the pattern of rings on the cut surface. Count the number of rings as carefully as you can: it is not always easy when you get close to the centre. Each ring of wood was formed during one year of the tree's growth, so by counting these annual rings you can tell how old the tree was when it was felled. Trees growing by themselves – in parks, for example – grow more quickly than trees in the woods because they have no competition. Their annual rings are broader than those of woodland trees. Notice the shoots already springing from the stump just a few months after it was cut.

Flowers, Fruits and Seeds

identification. Some of the easiest to recognize are the sharply pointed buds of the beech and the velvety black buds of the ash. Look at the twigs as well and see whether there are any little scars showing where the previous year's leaves fell. These scars are very obvious in the horse chestnut.

Tree Reproduction

Apart from the pines and other conifers, all our trees produce flowers. But not all the flowers are as obvious as those of the horse chestnut below. They often have no petals and no scent and they are pollinated by the wind. The hazel is a good example. Look for its long yellow catkins scattering pollen very

From Flower to Fruit

The horse chestnut originally came from Greece and is more common in parks and gardens than in woods. It is planted for its beautiful flowers (right). These are pollinated by bumble bees (below). After pollination the pistil of each flower swells to

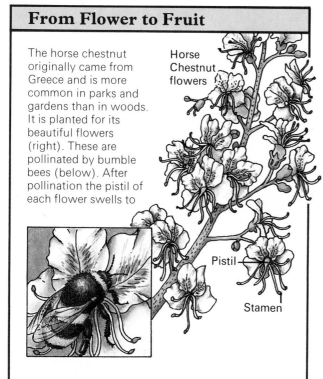

Horse Chestnut flowers

Pistil

Stamen

form the familiar prickly green fruit (below right). The fruit dries and splits when it is ripe to reveal the shiny brown seed that we call a conker. There are sometimes two conkers in each fruit. These large seeds have no special mechanism for dispersal.

Plant a fresh conker in a flower pot filled with rich soil. Keep it moist and you will soon see the seedling horse chestnut tree appear.

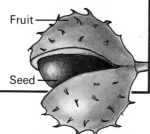

Fruit

Seed

Seeds and Fruits

The fruits of sycamore and elm are among many with 'wings'. Drop some from an upstairs window on a windy day and measure the distance they travel before landing. Beech nuts are protected in spiky cases at first, but these split open when they are ripe. You might see squirrels taking some away and burying them. Mice love blackberries. They eat the pips and flesh. Look for their stores of other fruits and seeds around the roots of trees.

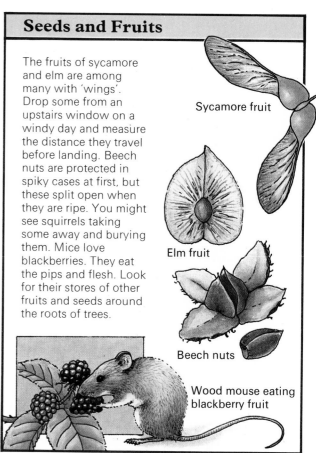

Sycamore fruit

Elm fruit

Beech nuts

Wood mouse eating blackberry fruit

early in the spring, long before the leaves open. The catkins consist only of male flowers. The female flowers, which are the ones that produce the nuts, look just like buds, but if you look carefully you will see tiny tufts of red hairs at the tip. These tufts are the stigmas, waiting to catch the pollen drifting in the breeze.

The ash and the elm also flower before their leaves open. Oak and beech produce their catkins at the same time as the leaves. Look for the flowers on other woodland trees and make drawings of them in your notebook.

Seed Dispersal

When the flowers have been pollinated they begin to swell up and form the fruits. The seeds develop inside the fruits. When the fruits and their seeds are ripe they are dispersed or scattered by the wind or by various animals. In this way the seeds get distributed over a wide area and some of them get a chance to grow into new trees. Look for seedling trees in the woods. They crop up all over the place, but you will notice that they never grow very big if they are under mature trees. Only those that spring up in a clearing – perhaps where an old tree has fallen – can grow properly. Eventually one outgrows the others and replaces the tree that fell.

Fleshy or juicy fruits, like cherries and crab apples, attract birds and other animals. The fruit is eaten, but the hard seeds are often spat out to grow where they fall. Some seeds are, of course, swallowed with the fleshy bit of the fruit, but this doesn't always mean that they are destroyed. Many pass right through the animals, and they often germinate even better after this treatment. Hard fruits, such as hazel nuts and acorns, attract squirrels and other animals who crack the shells to get at the seeds inside. They eat thousands of seeds and this might seem rather wasteful for the trees. But remember that the animals bury a lot of nuts as well, and they don't always remember where these stores are. Some of the buried seeds can then grow into new trees. A tree may produce many thousands of seeds during its life, and only one has to survive to replace the parent tree one day. Gather as many different woodland fruits as you can. Examine them to work out how each is dispersed and to find out what animals, if any, are involved in scattering each species.

Woodland Layers

A mature woodland of oak or ash has four fairly distinct layers. The trees themselves form the top layer, which is known as the canopy. Try to work out the height of the canopy when exploring the woodlands – see page 8. The shrub layer comes next. It includes hawthorn, blackthorn, hazel, holly and many other species. This layer is especially thick near the edge of the wood where there is more light. Underneath the shrub layer comes the field layer, consisting of the ferns and numerous flowering plants. Most of the flowers, such as violets and primroses, appear early in the year before the trees blot out too much light. The lowest

Making Leaf Rubbings

Strong thin paper

Soft pencil

Hornbeam leaf

Make a permanent record of leaf shapes by leaf-rubbing. Pick a fresh, unchewed leaf and cover it with a clean sheet of paper. Holding it firmly in place, rub over the whole leaf area with a soft pencil. The shape of the leaf and its veins is transferred to the paper. You could use a green pencil for a natural effect – or browns and yellows for autumn colours. Label the rubbing with the name of the tree and paste it into your notebook.

woodland layer is the ground layer which contains the mosses and liverworts and large numbers of toadstools. But the most important component of the ground layer is its carpet of dead leaves. Each of the four layers supports its own collection of animals, although some of the larger animals regularly move from one layer to another.

A Continuous Cycle

The leaves that fall in autumn are soon attacked by fungi and they start to rot. Collect a handful of dead leaves from the woodland floor and look for the branching white threads of the fungi. They grow all over the leaves and take food from them. The leaves gradually crumble away, and as they decay they give minerals back to the soil. More minerals are released when the fungi die. The minerals can be taken up by the roots of the trees and other plants and in this way there is a continuous re-cycling of the woodland material – from soil

The Woodland Floor

Above: These tawny grisette toadstools, forcing their way through the mosses and leaf litter, have sprung from a huge network of fungal threads – part of the complex living community of the woodland floor.

to tree, to soil again. Dead wood is recycled in just the same way.

Although fungi are very important in the breakdown of woodland materials, many other organisms are involved as well. Microscopic bacteria play a big part, and so do the hordes of insects and mites that live and feed among the leaf litter.

Autumn Toadstools

The fungal threads that you see spreading through the dead leaves are mostly the early stages of toadstools. They spend most of the year soaking up food from the leaves, and when they have absorbed enough they form the toadstools, which are their reproductive bodies. Look under some toadstools and you will find either lots of gills, spreading out like the spokes of a wheel, or a spongy surface with thousands of tiny pores. The gills and the

Making Spore Prints

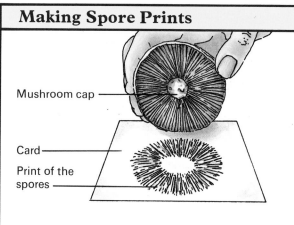

Mushroom cap

Card

Print of the spores

To get some idea of the vast numbers of spores scattered by toadstools, lay a cap on a piece of paper and leave it for a few hours. Lift it carefully to see the spore print where millions of tiny spores have fallen on to the paper. It is best to cover the cap with a basin while the print is being made because the slightest draught can disturb the spore pattern. Use dark paper for white-spored species.

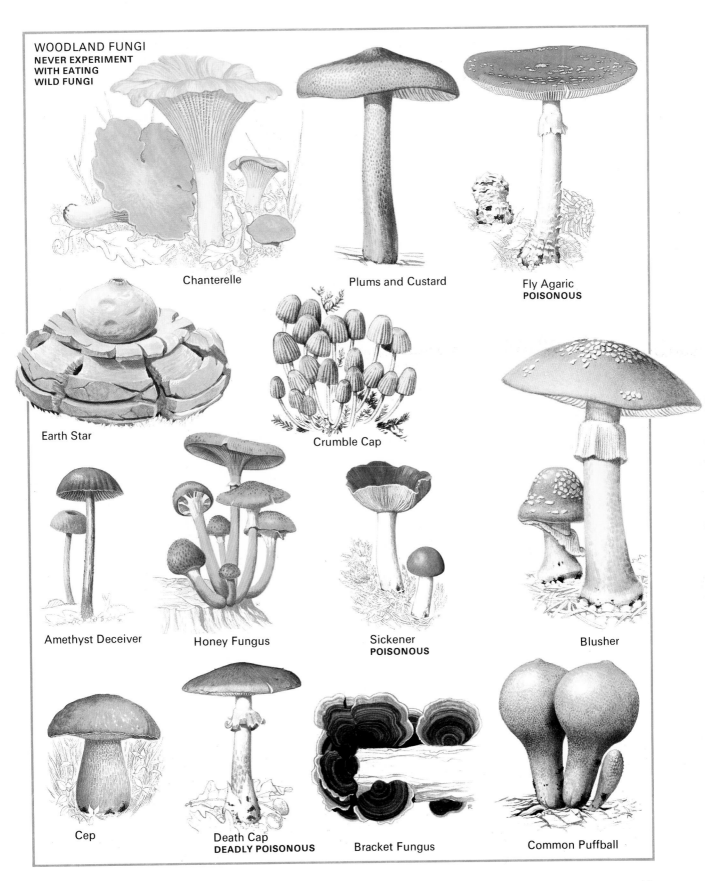

WOODLAND FUNGI
**NEVER EXPERIMENT
WITH EATING
WILD FUNGI**

Chanterelle

Plums and Custard

Fly Agaric
POISONOUS

Earth Star

Crumble Cap

Amethyst Deceiver

Honey Fungus

Sickener
POISONOUS

Blusher

Cep

Death Cap
DEADLY POISONOUS

Bracket Fungus

Common Puffball

Insects on the Woodland Floor

linings of the pores produce millions of minute spores which blow away in the wind. If they fall in suitable places they grow into new threads to start the sequence all over again. Look for earthstars and club-shaped puffballs. These fungi throw out their spores when disturbed. Drop a small twig on to one and watch the spores come out like a puff of smoke.

The Life of the Wood Ant

If you visit pinewoods or relatively dry oakwoods between spring and late autumn you might well meet the wood ants. These large reddish brown ants build huge nest mounds with pine needles and other plant debris. Many thousands of ants live in a single nest, and if you keep very quiet you can actually hear them rustling the dead leaves as they scurry over the woodland floor.

Wood ants don't sting, but they will bite and squirt formic acid at you if you annoy them. If you wear wellington boots and spray these with a good insect repellent, you can get right up to the nest and the ants won't bother you. Watch the army of worker ants bringing

The Quick-growing Stinkhorn

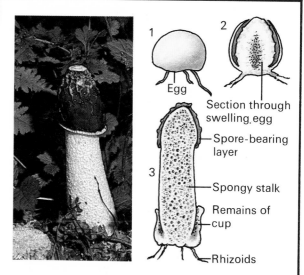

1 Egg

2 Section through swelling egg

Spore-bearing layer

3 Spongy stalk

Remains of cup

Rhizoids

You will smell the stinkhorn in the woods long before you see this strange toadstool. Starting from the 'egg' stage, the spongy spike can grow to 15 centimetres in an hour. A fresh stinkhorn has a slimy cap covered with spores. Flies are attracted by the smell and feed on the slime. They pick up spores on their feet and carry them off to grow elsewhere.

The Wood Ants

Wood ant nests are often built around old tree stumps (below). The mound containing many tunnels and chambers is made largely of plant debris, but the ants hate 'foreign' material. Put some cocktail sticks on to a mound and watch the ants drag them away (right).

CROSS-SECTION OF A NEST

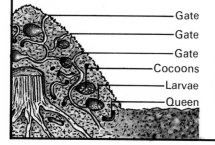

Gate
Gate
Gate
Cocoons
Larvae
Queen

food to the nest. All kinds of insects are dragged along – if they are too heavy the ants cut them up first. Many of the insects are caught in the trees and foresters like to have the ants around because they destroy so many pests. In some countries the wood ants are protected by law for this reason. As well as insects, the ants collect lots of honeydew which oozes out of aphids. It has been estimated that the workers of a large colony may collect 50 kilogrammes of honeydew in one summer. Watch the ants bring building materials to the mound and tug them right to the top. But they won't thank you for helping them: any material that you throw on will be immediately dragged down again and hauled right away from the nest.

The mound is only part of the nest. There are many chambers and tunnels right under the ground. Many queens live here, busily laying eggs throughout the summer. The workers feed the grubs here as well. Mating flights take place in early summer, with most of the new queens returning to their own nests after mating. The ants all hibernate for the winter in the deepest part of the nest. The mound sinks at this time of the year and has to be rebuilt in the spring.

Life in the Leaf Litter

The leaf litter that covers the woodland floor provides food and shelter for an astonishing variety of small animals. Two ways of finding these creatures – the pitfall trap and the Tullgren funnel – are described below. An even simpler method is to spread a handful of moist leaf litter over a large sheet of paper and search through it with a lens. A torch will help if you actually do this in the woods. Count the number of animals you can find in a handful of litter. For every one you find there will be many more that you don't see, for many of the animals are extremely tiny.

The springtails are usually the most noticeable creatures in this miniature world because they get very agitated and leap all over the place when disturbed. They are primitive wingless insects which feed on decaying leaves. With your lens, you might just be able to make out a forked spring at the hind end. When released by the springtail, it flicks the insect forwards. Look for mites as

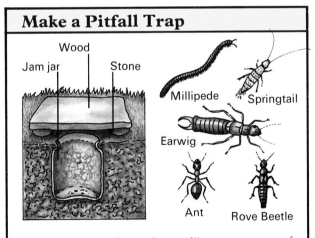

Make a Pitfall Trap

The simple trap shown here will capture many of the small creatures that roam the woodland floor at night. Make sure that the rim of the jar is absolutely level with the ground, and then the animals will crawl straight in. The cover keeps out the rain. Empty the trap in the morning. Some of the commonly captured animals are shown here.

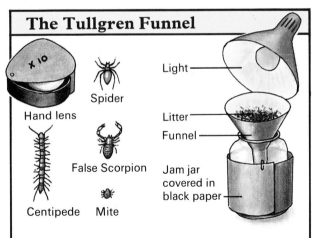

The Tullgren Funnel

Many minute animals live in moist leaf litter. You can find them with the apparatus shown here. Put some litter in the funnel and shine the light on it for a few hours. To avoid the heat and the dryness the animals burrow deeper into the litter. Many fall into the jar below. Line it with some damp blotting paper to keep them alive until you can examine them with a hand lens.

Mosses and Liverworts

well. Globular ones with spiky legs are very common. They feed by sucking the juices from decaying leaves and from fungal threads. The red velvet mites are carnivorous, but the most fascinating of the predatory creatures in the leaf litter are the false scorpions. Far too small to harm us, they use their pink claws to catch and poison mites and other tiny prey.

Mosses and Liverworts

These small flowerless plants generally grow in damp places and often form thick cushions or mats on the woodland floor. In really damp woods they even grow on the trees. Mosses have both slender creeping stems and short upright ones, clothed with very small leaves. Their cushion-like and mat-like growth helps to hold moisture around the delicate leaves. At certain times of the year they send out slender stalks topped by spore capsules that look like miniature pepper-pots. Spores are

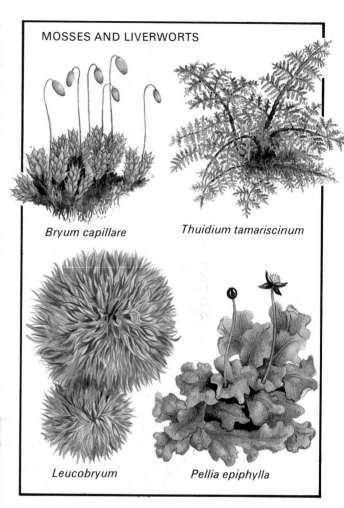

MOSSES AND LIVERWORTS

Bryum capillare

Thuidium tamariscinum

Leucobryum

Pellia epiphylla

Investigate a Moss

Use your lens to examine moss spore capsules. Each has a sort of pixie-hood at first, but this falls as the capsule ripens. Look at the end of a ripe capsule. It is like a tiny pepper-pot. Notice the tiny holes through which the minute spores escape. They open in dry weather and close in the wet.

Ripe capsule with hood about to fall

Open capsule (spores dispersed)

Stalk

Swan-necked Thread Moss

scattered in dry weather and those that reach suitably moist places will grow into new mosses. You can grow some yourself by shaking ripe capsules over some damp peat in a plastic box. Keep the box closed and the spores will soon produce a mat of greenish threads from which the mosses will sprout.

There are many different kinds of mosses. The fern-like *Thuidium* (above) is easy to recognize, and you should be able to pick out the greyish green spongy cushions of *Leucobryum* on the woodland floor. The bright green capsules help to identify *Bryum capillare*. Other mosses may not be as easy to identify. You will need a good lens to look at the shapes of their leaves and the help of detailed guide books.

Liverworts like even damper places than mosses. Many of them look just like mosses, but they have much simpler spore capsules that split right open and look like stars when they are ripe. But some liverworts look more like seaweeds. Look for these on the banks of shady woodland streams. *Pellia* (left) is a very common example. Lift up a piece and see the very simple roots that anchor it to the ground. Some liverworts carry little cups full of detachable buds. Raindrops falling into the cups splash the buds out and each can grow into a new plant.

The Field Layer

Flowering plants and ferns make up the woodland field layer. Most of the plants are soft-stemmed herbaceous species that die down in the autumn and send up new shoots in the spring. Many of the flowers grow from underground bulbs or tubers – a well-known bulbous species is the bluebell.

Like the shrub layer, the field layer is poorly developed in beechwoods and other dense woodlands and it is not found at all in mature conifer plantations. It reaches its greatest development in lightly grazed woodland clearings and places where trees have fallen and light is let in. There is also a very rich field layer in the woods which are regularly coppiced (see page 4). There are always some open areas in coppiced woodland in which flowers can flourish. As the new

Below: Foxgloves grow tall in an overgrown woodland clearing with elder bushes in flower behind them. Both of these plants spring up rapidly when trees are felled.

Woodland Flowers

coppice shoots grow up and shade the field layer some plants die, but others remain 'ticking over' without flowering until the coppice is cut some years later. After a year of sunlight, during which they build up food reserves, the plants flower again in profusion.

The kinds of flowers that grow in the field layer depend very much on the type of soil and the amount of moisture it holds. In pedunculate oakwoods, for example, where the soil is deep and rich, you could find bugle, primroses, yellow archangel, woodruff and early purple orchids, together with large patches of dog's mercury in which very little else can grow. The dog's mercury is a dark green plant, up to about 40 centimetres high, with inconspicuous spikes of greenish flowers in spring. You might mistake it for stinging nettles at first, but its leaves are smoother and more rounded. Dog's mercury tolerates shade reasonably well and can actually grow under beeches if they are not too dense. As the leaves of the trees grow and cast more shade, the dog's mercury leaves produce more chlorophyll and become darker. This helps them to make the best use of the available light. Many other field layer plants darken in this way during the summer.

The field layer of a sessile oakwood generally has fewer species than that of the pedunculate oakwood because the soil is shallower and not so rich. Common species include foxglove, wood sorrel and common cow-wheat. The latter is able to tolerate more shade than most plants and actually puts out its flowers, looking like spindly yellow snapdragons, in the middle of summer when the woodland canopy is at its densest. Bluebells also thrive on the shallow soils, but they don't like shade and they die down by mid-summer, after storing up most of the food that they need for the next spring.

Use a good guide book to help you to identify the flowers that you find in the woodlands. Write their names in your notebook and make a note of the kinds of woods in which you found them and the time of year. What is the soil like? You will find that most plants have definite preferences

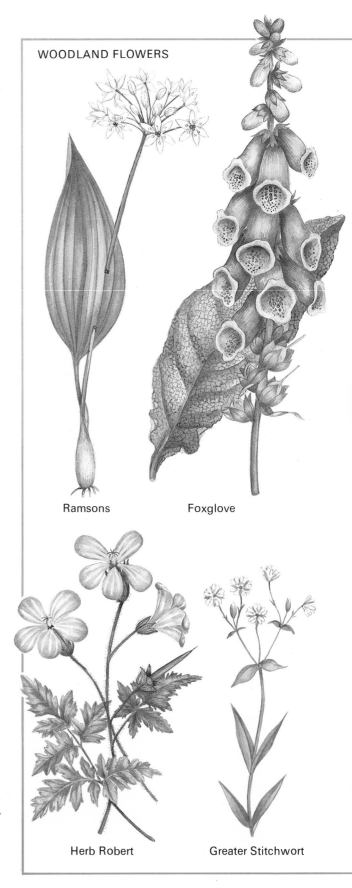

WOODLAND FLOWERS

Ramsons   Foxglove

Herb Robert   Greater Stitchwort

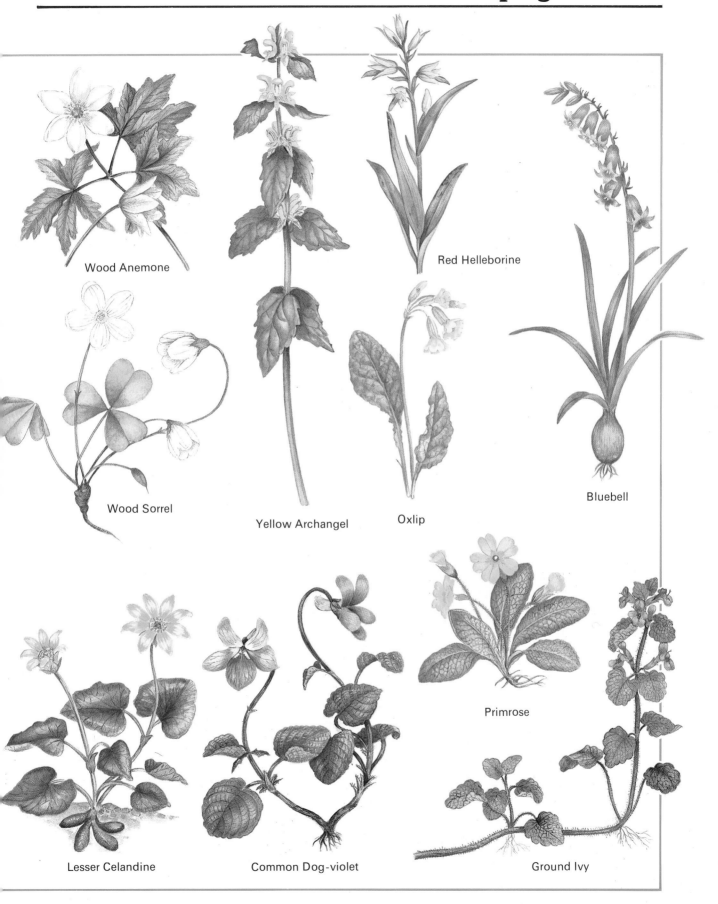

Wood Anemone

Red Helleborine

Wood Sorrel

Yellow Archangel

Oxlip

Bluebell

Primrose

Lesser Celandine

Common Dog-violet

Ground Ivy

Ferns

regarding the soil, but some occur in all kinds of woodlands. The wood anemone and herb robert are among these wide-ranging species.

Have a look at the brambles in the woods. Although they can use their hooked prickles to scramble over other shrubs, they often form thick carpets on the woodland floor and can be taken as part of the field layer. Notice how the tips of the branches take root when they touch the ground. The plants don't flower much when growing in the wood in this way, so don't expect to find many blackberries.

Woodland Ferns

Ferns all need damp conditions to reproduce themselves and are much commoner in western regions of the British Isles, where rainfall is heavy, than in the east. In the wettest areas they often grow on the branches of the trees. The common polypody (opposite) is the commonest of our epiphytic or tree-growing ferns.

The male fern, pictured below, is often found on the woodland floor wherever conditions are reasonably damp. It has a short underground stem which sends up a cluster of

The Bird's Nest Orchid

The bird's nest orchid is one of a number of strange woodland flowers with no green colouring and no leaves. It can't make food in the normal way. Instead it absorbs ready-made food from dead and decaying leaves on the woodland floor. Because it does not need sunlight, this orchid can grow in very dark woods. Look for it in beech woods from May to July. It is one of the few flowering plants that can survive in the deep shade under the beeches. Even the flowers have no bright colour, but they smell quite sweetly of honey which attracts various small flies. The plant gets its name from its tangled cluster of roots, which resemble a small nest.

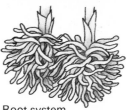

Root system

Growing Ferns from Spores

Look under fern fronds for the clusters of brown spore capsules. Those shown below belong to the male fern. Scatter some spores over moist sand or peat in a plastic box. Keep it covered and watch how the spores grow. They develop into heart-shaped plates called prothalli, and new ferns later grow from these. You will need your lens to look at the prothalli.

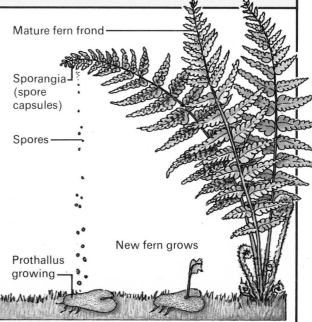

Mature fern frond

Sporangia (spore capsules)

Spores

Prothallus growing

New fern grows

large green leaves each spring. Notice how the leaves or fronds unfurl. This is typical of ferns, but not seen in any other group of plants. Look closely at the base of the fern and you will see the next year's leaves already tightly coiled there. Each leaf is divided into numerous small leaflets.

Ferns have no flowers and they reproduce by means of minute spores. If you brush against a fern in summer you might well find yourself covered with the powdery brown spores. Look under the fronds to see the clusters of spore capsules which release the spores. The capsules are arranged in different ways in different ferns.

The commonest fern is the bracken. This tall species has more or less triangular fronds which arise singly instead of in clusters as in the male fern and most other ferns. The young fronds look like little shepherds' crooks when they first push through the ground. This curving of the shoot protects the very delicate tissues at the tip. Bracken does not rely entirely on its spores for its spread and can thrive in much drier places than other ferns. It has a creeping underground stem that can extend more than a metre a year. The plant covers the ground in many sessile oakwoods and pinewoods and also spreads over huge areas of heathland. If you see it in the woods you can be sure that the soil is well drained, for the bracken cannot survive having its roots in water for long.

Look for other kinds of ferns on rocky woodland banks. Three common species are shown on the right. The hard fern carries its spores on special upright fronds which die when the spores have blown away. The hart's tongue doesn't look like a fern at all until you see the spore capsules under the leaves.

Woodland Insects

Examine any ten leaves from woodland trees and other plants in the summer: at least seven will probably show signs of insect attack. Holes in the middle suggest that they have been nibbled by beetles, while bits taken from the edges may be the work of beetles or caterpillars. Look under the leaves for aphids.

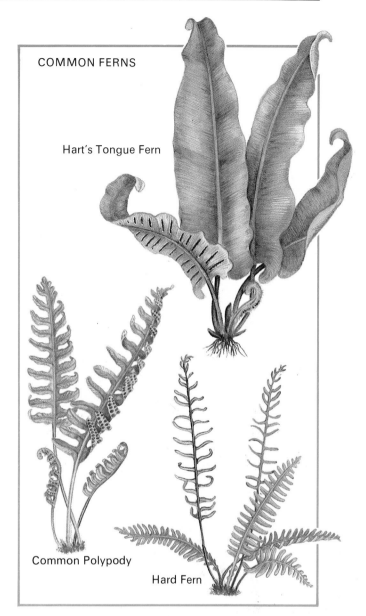

COMMON FERNS

Hart's Tongue Fern

Common Polypody

Hard Fern

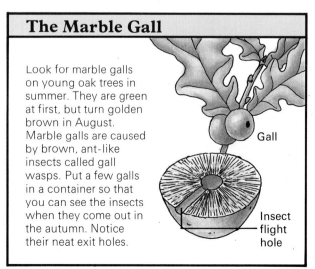

The Marble Gall

Look for marble galls on young oak trees in summer. They are green at first, but turn golden brown in August. Marble galls are caused by brown, ant-like insects called gall wasps. Put a few galls in a container so that you can see the insects when they come out in the autumn. Notice their neat exit holes.

Gall

Insect flight hole

Butterflies and Moths

Use a Beating Tray

A sharp knock will send lots of insects tumbling from the branches of trees and shrubs. You can catch them in a simple beating tray, made from part of an old sheet stretched over a light wooden frame or you can just lay a sheet on the ground. Keep a note of the insects you get from each kind of tree. The yellow-tail caterpillar (below) is often beaten from hawthorn in the spring.

Pale blotches may show where minute grubs have burrowed between the upper and lower leaf surfaces. The burrows are called leaf mines. Look for the long twisting mines on bramble leaves, excavated by the caterpillars of a tiny moth.

Keep your eyes open for plant galls as well. These strange growths are especially common on oak trees. There are many different kinds, each caused by a different kind of insect. But it is not just the leaves that are attacked: flowers and fruits and even the timber itself all provide food for insects. And then there are the many carnivorous insects in the wood, including the ladybirds and many other beetles. Look out for the delicate green lacewings which fly from many plants when disturbed. You might startle the oak bush-cricket, a pale green grasshopper-like insect that rests in the trees by day. It feeds on small caterpillars and other insects.

Moths and Butterflies

Moths generally fly at night and rest by day. Search the tree trunks for resting moths. Many are very well camouflaged to protect them from birds. Others prefer to hide amongst the leaves. Some woodland moths are pictured below. The speckled yellow and

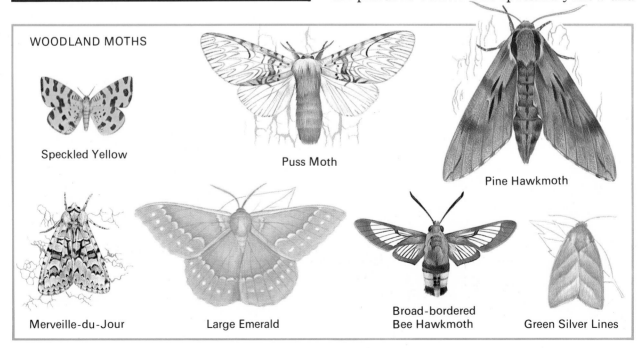

WOODLAND MOTHS

Speckled Yellow

Puss Moth

Pine Hawkmoth

Merveille-du-Jour

Large Emerald

Broad-bordered Bee Hawkmoth

Green Silver Lines

the broad-bordered bee hawkmoth fly in woodland clearings in the sunshine, but the others are nocturnal.

Butterflies are sun-loving insects and you must look for the woodland species in rides and clearings. They enjoy sunbathing on the leaves. Most of them take nectar from flowers, but the purple emperor prefers to drink honeydew deposited on the leaves by aphids. This striking butterfly spends most of its time flying around tall oak trees, although it sometimes comes down to drink from muddy pools and also has a liking for rotting meat. Collectors used to lure the butterfly to the ground by putting down a dead rabbit or other flesh.

WOODLAND BUTTERFLIES

male

Pearl-bordered Fritillary

British form

Southern European form

Speckled Wood

female

caterpillar

Silver-washed Fritillary

Ringlet

Purple Emperor

Lesser Purple Emperor

caterpillar

White Admiral

Woodland Birds

Woodland Birds

The birds are the most obvious of the woodland animals. You can't go into a wood without hearing them, even if you can't see them right away. A few of the many different kinds of woodland birds are pictured opposite. Some, like the golden oriole and the green woodpecker, are very easy to recognize. Some of the others are more difficult, but if you study the pictures you will soon learn the important features and be able to identify the birds when you spot them in the woods. Use a good guide book to help you with the many other birds you will see in the woods.

Bird Songs

Another way of identifying common birds in the woods is to learn their songs. You can buy or borrow recordings to help you, and then you will be able to impress your friends by telling them that there is a chiffchaff in the trees although you can't actually see it. The chiffchaff's song is actually an easy one to recognize: it sounds just like the bird's name repeated over and over again – *chiff-chaff-chiff-chaff-chiff-chaff*. This is, of course, how the bird got its name. Once you have heard the beautiful song of the nightingale on a recording you won't be able to mistake it in the woods. This drab brown bird sings by day as well as at night, but it is clearer at night when the other birds are quiet. Other easily recognized songs include those of the cuckoo and the woodpigeon. The latter has a rather soft five-note song with the second note long and loud and a distinct pause before the last two notes: *cu-cooo-coo——coo-coo*.

Male birds sing to defend their territories and to attract mates. Most birds also have other calls, shorter than their songs, which they use to call to their offspring or to warn of danger. The blackbird, for example, gives out a shrill *pink-pink-pink* when it is alarmed. Listen also for the rather strange drumming of the great spotted woodpecker as it hammers its beak on a dead branch like a pneumatic drill. This sound is used instead of a song to defend their territory and you will hear it mainly in the spring.

Bird Diets

Leaves are abundant in the woodlands, but very few birds actually eat leaves. The capercaillie of the northern coniferous forests is one of the few. It eats the shoots of pines and other conifers during the winter. Woodpigeons also eat lots of leaves, but these are usually stripped from the fields and not from the trees. Some finches, notably the bullfinch, feed on buds, but they don't eat mature leaves.

Fruits and seeds are much more important in the diets of woodland birds. Finches are essentially seed-eaters and they are equipped

Watching Birds

Birdwatcher

Jay

Binoculars are essential for every keen bird-watcher. They help you to pick out distinguishing marks and identify birds from a considerable distance. There are lots of different models, but if you are likely to do most of your birdwatching in the woods, where the light is often rather poor, you need a pair with good light-gathering power. This means a pair with fairly large objectives – the lenses furthest from your eyes. The larger these lenses, the more light they can pass to your eyes. But larger lenses are also heavy, so you must strike a balance. A pair marked 7 x 50 are good for night viewing and for woodland work. They magnify 7 times and the objectives are 50 mm across. Also fine for birdwatching are 8 x 30 and 8 x 40 binoculars, although the image might be a little dim in thick woodland. Be careful not to scratch the lenses on bushes and low branches.

WOODLAND BIRDS

Chiffchaff

Golden Oriole
male
female

Great Spotted Woodpecker

Green Woodpecker
male
female

Coal Tit

Nuthatch

Lesser
Spotted Woodpecker
female
male

Woodpigeon

Treecreeper

Crossbill
male
female

Goldcrest
female
male

Chaffinch
female
male
male
(winter)

Nightingale

Redpoll
female
male

with stout beaks for crushing the seeds. The hawfinch's beak is so strong that it can crack open a cherry stone with ease. The crossbill is one of the most interesting finches. It uses the crossed tips of its beak to winkle out the seeds from the cones of pines and other conifers. The bird eats almost nothing else. Look for cones that it has attacked: the cone scales have been levered apart and broken, and those of spruce cones have usually been split right down the centre. Jays eat all kinds of food but are particularly fond of acorns. If you watch them in autumn you can see them flying from the oakwoods with their beaks and throats bulging with acorns, which they bury in surrounding areas as winter stores.

Insects are the main diet of many other woodland birds. Most of the insect-eaters have slender beaks. Watch the treecreeper running up tree trunks and probing the bark for insects. The nuthatch feeds in a similar way but can walk down the trunk as well. It also uses its powerful beak to open nuts, wedging them in bark crevices before hammering them apart. Look for the broken shells still jammed in the bark. Woodpeckers do much the same, but remove the empty shells and drop them on the ground below so that they can use the same crevice over and over again. As well as nuts, the woodpeckers eat large numbers of insects which they dig out from dead and dying trunks.

Nests Everywhere

Birds build their nests everywhere from ground level to the tree-tops, although each species has its prefered sites. Tits, for example, like to nest in tree holes. A dense shrub layer provides excellent cover for many warblers, which often nest very close to the ground. The nightjar actually nests on the ground. It makes no real nest but lays its eggs in a slight hollow. The sitting bird is almost invisible against the background of fallen leaves and twigs

It is against the law to disturb nesting birds, but when you are sure that they have left their nests for good you can examine the nests to see what they are made of.

Below: A female sparrowhawk guards her nest in a spruce tree. She and her mate are incredibly agile as they chase other birds through the trees. They must catch several small birds each day to feed themselves and their growing chicks.

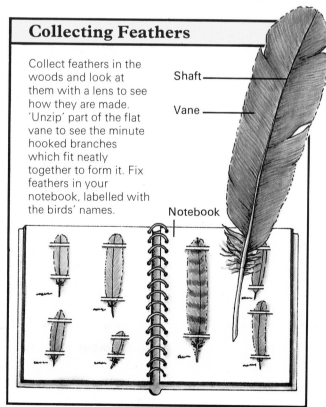

Collecting Feathers

Collect feathers in the woods and look at them with a lens to see how they are made. 'Unzip' part of the flat vane to see the minute hooked branches which fit neatly together to form it. Fix feathers in your notebook, labelled with the birds' names.

Shaft

Vane

Notebook

Woodland Mammals

Apart from the squirrels, most of our woodland mammals are active at night. Dusk and dawn are the best times to watch them in action, as long as you know where to look, but don't go to the woods alone. Deer are not difficult to find, especially the fallow deer. These live in fairly large herds and make conspicuous tracks through the woods. Look for their footprints in soft ground to show you where to go. They usually browse in clearings or along the edges of the woods, where you can watch them quite easily as long as you are careful about the wind direction. The wind must be blowing from the deer to you: if you approach from the wrong direction the animals will smell you and trot away before you get near enough to see them.

The flesh-eating mammals are more difficult to find and watch because most of them move about singly, but if you can find their homes and get in position before dusk you might see them come out. Badgers and foxes can be watched in this way. Badgers often romp about outside their burrows for a while, especially if they have cubs with them. A piece of red plastic fixed over your torch will enable you to observe these and other mammals because the animals' eyes are not very sensitive to the red light. Rarer mammals that you might be able to see in the woods are polecats, pine martens and wild cats. Lumps of meat or tinned pet food may attract them to your observation point, although none of these animals is really common. Look at their footprints after the animals have visited the bait. Stoats are often seen streaking across paths and clearings by day. Look for the black tip of the tail which distinguishes the stoat from its smaller cousin, the weasel.

Look out for other signs of animals: barbed wire around the woods is always worth examining for hairs left behind by mammals passing under or over the wire. The black and white hairs of the badger are easily identified, and so are the coarse hairs of deer. Other mammalian hairs can be identified, but only under a microscope. Piles of droppings will also give you clues about where to watch for the woodland mammals.

Right: The red squirrel is generally brick-red in summer, but greyer in winter, when it can be distinguished from the grey squirrel (above) by its ear tufts. Chewed cones and empty nut shells, often on tree stumps, show you where the squirrels have been eating.

Mammal Tracks

Mammal Tracks

A fox looks out from its den or earth. Foxes come out mainly at night. Look for their footprints (below) on muddy paths. They are similar to dog footprints but the two middle toes point inwards and they are much closer together. The surest sign of the fox, however, is its very strong smell.

A woodmouse explores a tree stump at night in search of food. The beech nuts in the picture will do very well. Notice the mouse's very large ears and eyes – both very necessary for finding its way and detecting danger at night. The animal also has a good sense of smell and uses its long whiskers to feel its way in the dark.

The common dormouse rarely ventures out by day. It feeds mainly in the bushes by night. It likes all kinds of fruits and seeds and here it is gnawing an unripe hazel nut – one of its favourite foods. Notice how the animal wraps its tail around a branch and uses it like an extra leg to cling firmly to the trees.

Making Plaster Casts

Plaster of Paris

Coil of paper held with paper clip

Badger print in the mud

Find a good clear footprint in the mud and surround it with a strip of thin card as shown above. Push the card well into the mud without disturbing the print. Mix some plaster of Paris in an old basin or large yoghurt pot and pour it into the circle of card. Leave it to set – about 20 minutes is usually long enough – and then dig it up. After washing, you will have a good cast of the animal's foot. You may need a little practice to get the mixture just right.

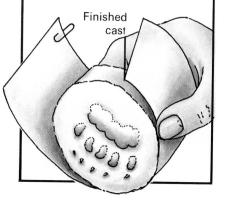

Finished cast

Badgers and Roe Deer

Watching Badgers

Big holes in woodland banks surrounded by lots of bare ground and scratched trees show you where badgers live, but you must go back at night to see the animals. Never go alone. Be in position, downwind of the holes, well before dusk and keep very quiet.

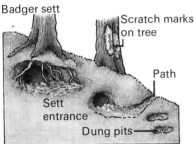

Badger sett

Scratch marks on tree

Path

Sett entrance

Dung pits

The Timid Roe Deer

The roe deer is the smallest of our native deer and, unlike most others, it does not live in herds. You will normally see just one at a time, or perhaps a small family group. Look for their footprints (below) in muddy paths. The animals are very shy and mainly nocturnal. You usually see them by accident, running rapidly away when you have disturbed their daytime rest. The animals are greyer in winter and then you can see the conspicuous white rump as they run. The males have antlers from late spring to late autumn and the antlers never have more than three points.

Roe deer footprint about one third natural size

Woodland Seasons

Spring

Bluebells carpet many beechwoods in the spring. Their leaves appear as winter turns to spring and the flowers follow in May, just as the beech leaves are beginning to open and cut off the light. The bluebell leaves continue to grow for another month or so, and then die away after pumping all their food into the bulbs ready for the next year. The best stands of flowers are to be found in the slightly more open areas where the leaves get more light and can make more food. Close to the beech trunks, where conditions are very shady and very dry in summer, there may be a few spindly bluebell plants, but they rarely flower in such places.

Summer

Throughout the summer the beech leaves are spread out so that they get the maximum amount of light to make food for the trees. Very little light reaches the ground. There are bright patches here and there, but they receive light only for short periods, when the sun can get through small chinks in the canopy, and few plants can grow there. Only in larger clearings, where a tree has fallen, can bracken and other plants thrive in the summer. Notice how the last autumn's leaves still carpet the ground. Their toughness, combined with the dryness of the woodland floor, means that they decay very slowly, so there are always plenty of dead leaves for you to shuffle through as you walk.

Autumn

Autumn is a beautiful time in the beechwoods, with the leaves taking on their wonderful golden and coppery colours. Food is being rapidly withdrawn from the leaves at this time and stored in the twigs and branches ready for the following spring. Thin corky layers develop between the twigs and the leaf stalks and gradually cut off all water supplies to the leaves. The autumn winds then gradually blow the leaves from the trees. Some light then reaches the ground, but much more important is the rain reaching the ground. Decay of the previous year's leaves speeds up and crops of toadstools spring up on the woodland floor.

Winter

Even in winter there is quite a lot of shade in the beechwood. Look up at the branches and see how the twigs form a dense lattice. Look closely at one of the lower branches to see the narrow pointed buds so characteristic of the beech. At the base of the trunk you can see how the shallow roots spread out in all directions, sucking up all the available moisture and making the soil very dry. A few mosses grow here and there, especially on banks where they are above the carpet of dead leaves. Notice how smooth the beech bark is – another characteristic feature of this tree. It is often stained green by algae, especially on the shadier (northern) side of the trunk.

Index

Page numbers in *italics* refer to illustrations

A
Acorn 4, *6*, 11, 26
Alder *6*
Amethyst Deceiver *13*
Aphid 15, 21
Ash 5, *6*, 10

B
Badger *3*, 27, 28, *29*
Bark 5, 6–7, *9*, *31*
Beating tray 22
Beech *4*, 5, *6*, 10, *10*
Beechwoods *4*, 5, 17, 20, 30–31
Beetles 2, *15*, 21, 22
Binoculars 4, *24*
Birch *6*, 7
Birds 4, 5, 11, 24–26
Bird songs 24
Bird's Nest Orchid 20
Blackberry *10*, 20
Blackbird 24
Bluebell 5, 17, 18, *19*, *30*
Blusher *13*
Bracken 2, *2*, 21, 30
Bracket Fungi 2, *3*, *13*
Bramble *see* Blackberry
Bryum capillare 16, *16*
Bumble Bee *10*
Butterflies 2, *3*, 23, *23*

C
Canopy 11, 30
Capercaillie 24
Caterpillars *3*, 21, 22–23
Catkins *6*, 7, 10
Centipede *15*
Cep *13*
Chaffinch 2, *3*, 25
Chanterelle *13*
Chiffchaff 24, *25*
Common Cow-wheat 18
Common Polypody 20, *21*
Conifers 2, 4, 5, *6*, 7, *7*, 10, 17
Conker *10*
Coppicing 4, 5, 17, 18
Country code 2
Crossbill 25, 26
Crumble Cap *13*
Cuckoo 24
Cuttings *9*

D
Death Cap *13*
Deer 2, *2*, 27, *29*
Dog's Mercury 18
Dormouse 28

E
Earthstar *13*, 14
Earwig *15*
Elder *17*
Elm 7, 10, *10*

F
Fallow Deer 2, *2*
False Scorpion *15*, 16

Feathers *26*
Ferns 2, *2*, 11, 17, 20–21
Finches 24, *25*, 26
Flowers 2–3, 6–7, 10, *10*, 17–20
Fly Agaric *13*
Fox 27, *28*
Foxglove *17*, 18, *18*
Fruits 6–7, 10–11, 24
Fungi 2, *3*, 7, 11, 12–14

G
Galls *21*, 22
Goldcrest *25*
Golden Oriole 24, *25*

H
Hand lens 4, *15*
Hard Fern 21, *21*
Hart's Tongue 21, *21*
Hawthorn *6*, 11
Hazel 4, 5, *6*, 10, 11
Holly 7, 11
Honeydew *15*, 21
Honey Fungus *13*
Hornbeam *6*, 11
Hornet 2, *3*
Horse Chestnut *6*, 7, 10

I, J, K
Insects 2, 12, 14–16, 21–23, 26
Jay 2, *3*, *24*, 26
Kestrel 2, 4

L
Larch *6*, 7
Leaves 4, 5, 6–7, 11, *11*, 12, 15–16, 24, 30, 31
Leucobryum 16, *16*
Lime *6*
Liverworts 11, 16–17

M
Maple *6*
Mice 5, *10*, 28
Millipede *15*
Mites 15, *15*, 16
Mosses 11, 16, *16*, 31
Moths 22–23
Mushrooms 12, *13*

N
Nests 14, *14*, 15, 26
Nightingale 24, *25*
Nightjar 26
Nuthatch *3*, 25, 26
Nuts *6*, 7, 10–11, 26, *28*

O
Oaks 2, *3*, 4, *4*, 5, *6*, 10, *21*, 22
Oakwoods 4–5, 14, 18, 26
Orchids 18, *20*

P
Pellets 5
Pellia 16, 17
Pine Marten 27
Pines 5, *7*, 10, 24, 26
Pinewoods 5, *5*, 7, 14

Pitfall trap 15, *15*
Plums and Custard *13*
Polecat 27
Primrose 11, 18, *19*
Puffball *13*, 14
Purple Emperor Butterfly 23, *23*

R
Redpoll *25*
Roe Deer *29*

S
Seeds 10–11, 24
Shrew 5
Shrubs 11, 26
Sickener *13*
Sparrowhawk 26
Spores 12, 14, 16, *20*, 21
Springtail 15, *15*
Spruce *6*, 7
Squirrels *3*, 11, 27, *27*
Stinkhorn 14
Stoat *3*, 27
Swan-necked Thread Moss 16
Sweet Chestnut 7, *7*
Sycamore *6*, 10

T
Tawny Owl 5
Thuidium 16, *16*
Tits 2, *3*, 25, 26
Toadstools 12–14, 31
Tracks 27, *28*, *29*
Treecreeper 25, 26
Tree rings *9*
Tullgren funnel 15, *15*

V
Violet 11, *19*
Vole 4, 5

W
Warblers 26
Weasel 27
Wild Cat 27
Wild Cherry *6*, 7
Wood Ant 14–15
Wood mouse *10*, 28
Woodpeckers *3*, 24, *25*, 26
Woodpigeon 24, *25*
Wood Sorrel 18, *19*

Y
Yellow Archangel 18, *19*
Yew 7

Editor: Vanessa Clarke
Designer: Ben White
Illustrators: Wendy Bramall, Martin Camm, Jeane Colville, Alan Male, Bernard Robinson, Ann Winterbotham and David Wright.
Cover Design: Pinpoint Design Company
Picture Research: Jackie Cookson

Photographs: page 4 Heather Angel; 26 Nature Photographers; 27 Nature Photographers; 28 NHPA/Stephen Dalton *top*, Heather Angel *centre*, Nature Photographers *bottom*; 29 NHPA/N.J. Dennis *top*, Nature Photographers *bottom*; 30 Heather Angel *top*; all other photographs: Michael Chinery.

First published in 1985 by Kingfisher Books Limited, Elsley Court, 20-22 Great Titchfield Street London W1P 7AD
A Grisewood & Dempsey Company

Text Copyright © Michael Chinery 1985
Illustrations Copyright © Kingfisher Books Ltd 1985

BRITISH LIBRARY CATALOGUING IN PUBLICATION DATA
Chinery, Michael
    Woodlands,– (Exploring the countryside)
    1. Natural history–Great Britain– Juvenile literature
    2. Forest fauna–Great Britain– Juvenile literature
    I. Title   II. Series
    574.941   QH137
ISBN: 0 86272 147 4

Typeset by Southern Positives and Negatives (SPAN) Lingfield, Surrey.
Printed in Italy by Vallardi Industrie Grafiche, Milan